LEARNOLOGY

MEDITATIONS ON THE MEANING OF LEARNING

MIGUEL PANÃO

COMBOOKS

For Marta, Sara, David and Raquel.
With all of you I learned how to exist.

CONTENTS

INTRODUCTION

"Life is long if you know how to use it."
SENECA

Aware of it or not, we all sense the meaning of learning as *the* most transformative experience of every human being. I believe *learnology* to be more than a science aimed at acquiring knowledge and understanding. It is the logic (*logos*) behind a life oriented toward learning. I also believe that human potential flourishes from the experience of daily learning. Learning is not a task we perform to become someone. Learning is our being and becoming. If learning became the ultimate outcome of why we get up every single day, we might experience human evolution in real-time.

Learning is the reason why we are on this planet. Surviving was only the first stage of learning, but we came far from a humble beginning. However, the mindless gaze of many people wandering through the streets with their heads bowed at the majesty of their screens makes me wonder if we have forgotten our origins.

We live in the age of a massive information flow, giving us the feeling of knowing all when there is to know and be content. But how much do we understand of what we know? We sense the lack of time going deeper into our inner self-sense of worth, but we have enough time if we learn how to use it, increasing our learning capital.

We began as an individual among many, but the moment we shared what we learned with another individual, we became a community, a family. We discovered the secret of legacy and imprinted unexpected learning dynamics in this world. But I wonder if we are aware of such uniqueness.

We need the next step in human evolution. Learning brought us to where we are today. When we rediscover the love for learning, we will set in motion a narrative leading us to an evolutionary step with a profound and relational sense of self and belonging. It is time to wake up, again and again, to live in the awareness of why we learn.

For a year, I thought about the polyhedral side of learning with its different facets and nuances. I wrote about it as an inner search, more than anything else, and realized how learning is experiential.

I offer the thoughts in this book, hoping you may find in them a small inspiration to start a lifelong learning path, unique as you are unique. When I wrote these meditations on learning, I thought of the human heart inside every person from every generation because I believe learning to be the sole thing we do from the cradle to the grave. Each word is a facet of polyhedric learning, driving the dynamics of experiential learning. Words inspire these short meditations. You may read the one that best expresses what you are living while learning or the one that captures your attention and intrigues you. Also, consider all blank spaces as a canvas to write your own words.

I hope you find them a humble beginning on your path toward long-life learning, inspiring you to discover the beauty of making learning the reason why you breathe.

ACCOUNTABILITY

We can learn by ourselves or learn with others. But what does it mean to learn with others?

It can mean we learn together, helping each other. Or it can mean we count on others while we are learning. The latter is accountability. Someone who helps us stay on track with our learning or be ourselves, the accountability partner helping others.

Accountability shows how deeply relational learning is. But I wonder if people are willing to do it. Nobody seems to have time for anything. And helping others not only comes from the heart, but also from the way we manage time and attention. Or, even willing to let others be part of our time and attention.

We may think that spending time helping others is a waste, but if you put yourself in the skin of the other, would you believe the same?

My experience is to embrace flexibility whenever a friend, colleague, or family asks our help when learning something while being free to say, "Not right now, but how soon could we meet?" A learning opportunity for those we help can be a learning opportunity for ourselves because relational learning is reciprocal. And we never lose time and attention when we learn.

ALWAYS

$\mathcal{W}$e learn when we fail, pay attention, let curiosity move our minds, recognize with humility how much more there is to know, and show up for learning every second, minute, hour, day, month, year, and always.

Knowing is having a critical viewpoint of the information available.

Learning is transforming our lives with what we know.

But what I see in the streets, buses, and even at the University is people thinking they are consuming information to acquire knowledge and learn, but, instead, they're being consumed in their time and attention, feeling entertained. These people are giving their precious time and attention to others in exchange for a dopamine rush. I see addiction and wasted learning potential.

There is so much more with a few tiny tweaks in your life which depend only on you.

Moments of pause.

Moments of decluttering.

Moments of exercise.

Moments of reading or writing.

Moments of resting.

Moments of listening in silence.

And the more you practice these and other valuable moments of learning, in time, you'll understand the unique learning superpower you have inside and within your reach. And how much you can learn with every single moment in your life.

AWARENESS

While reading Cal Newport's book on *Digital Minimalism*, I learned about the reality of companies building apps to - literally- hack your brain. Have you noticed? Me neither.

We don't even realize we're being hacked at all because we don't even know what *brain hacking* is. It is simple. Brain hacking in today's digital era is craving to check your phone looking for anything new constantly. This "anything new" is, physically, a surge of dopamine demanded by our addictive brain.

The antidote is free and with you all the time: *awareness*.

If we learn to become increasingly aware of what apps are - *attention-leechers* - we begin to thoroughly analyze their true value in our lives and choose to use those really worthy of our time and attention.

ALTER-LISTEN

*E*very person speaking to us is an opportunity to learn. If not explicitly, we learn to listen.

One of my main flaws was listening to others. While someone was speaking to me, my mind was a storm of ideas about what she was saying. I would easily interrupt others and begin speaking instead of listening. Often, my closest friends would say I should listen more and better. They were right.

The moment you empty yourself from any thoughts to actually listen to someone else, a world of possibilities opens in front of you.

The other is a world to discover in front of me. If I learn to listen, I develop one of the greatest *learnabilities* of today.

The learnability to pay attention.

And this is valid whether the other is boring or not.

"When you pay attention to boredom, it gets unbeliev-ably interesting."

(Jon Kabat-Zinn, educator)

Seize every listening opportunity today because each will make you a better listener. Listening to others is one of the best ways of growing an attentive mindset and developing your learning mind.

ALTER-RE-LEARN

We all forget some of the things we learned throughout life. But when others share something we learn and forget, here's your chance to re-learn and rejoice.

Why re-learn and not remember? Learning is more than memorizing. It is an experience including memory, feelings, actions, and thinking.

Re-learning should be, above all, re-experiencing. Think about helping a friend or child when they're learning a topic for the first time. A topic you learned a long time ago. Don't you feel the joy of re-experiencing what learning is? And often, due to our life experience, it seems you re-learn the same thing with a different and deeper level of understanding.

Re-learning with those who learn is an opportunity to grow our curious mindset we should never miss.

ALTRUISTIC

Think about the work you do without being paid. If someone says it's foolish, never mind. Altruism will always be beyond reason and at your grasp.

Of rescuers of Jews during World War II, the psychologist Eva Fogelman said

> "Learned altruistic behavior, seeing all people as equals, gave the rescuers the ability to transcend the propaganda against the Jews and to see them as human beings just like themselves. They took the responsibility to help because they knew that unless they did something, that person would die."

When we learn altruism, we grow our degree of empathy and compassion toward others. We learn to persuade instead of obligate. We overcome the fear of personal risk when trying to do the right thing. And we can help others by word and example.

Altruism is not innate but developed through our relationships, according to one study by Rodolfo Barragan and Carol Dweck[1]. Therefore, it's not natural but learned. In fact, we become altruistic learners if we practice a gesture toward others every day. We'll improve the world around us and beyond our time.

AUTONOMY

It is likely to be the best and most difficult thing to achieve with anything you learn.

When you're autonomous, you do anything by yourself. You do not copy or let others do it for you.

When you're autonomous, you'll fail and fail again until you fail better (Samuel Beckett), but you'll eventually succeed with your resilient mindset, wholeheartedness, and bare hands.

When you're autonomous, you do it for yourself, but you're not by yourself. Our autonomy is interrelated with other autonomies, and the uniqueness each perspective brings to any problem leads to truly creative work.

We are *Learning-Minds*.

We are rational and creative, but what distinguishes our species on this planet is our ability to learn and share this knowledge throughout generations. This is only possible because we communicate. And communication is not only about speaking, but especially about listening—attentive listening.

The result of this communication through attentive listening leads to learning. Our mind learns when we pay attention. We may not be fully aware of this, but our evolution only came through learning, as I read in an article from the September issue of Scientific American (2018) on "What made us unique." This is why I wonder if we are aware of being learning minds.

Being a learning mind means paying attention, always being curious, striving for resilience, welcoming failure with humility, and finding courage in vulnerability. Our species will continue to evolve if we learn until that last dying breath. The implications of this awareness can be profound but reduced to nothing unless we live them every moment of every day.

CARING

The latest research in psychology confirms we need a break to avoid a break in our productivity. Efficiency is the ratio between what you produce with the number of resources available. Doing things corresponds to your resources. Thus, you understand if you produce the same by doing less, you're more efficient and more productive. Why doing less counts more?

We have four basic health perspectives in life: physical, mental, spiritual, and relational. And all are intrinsically interconnected.

Taking care of your body allows you to pay more attention and learn more. It implies exercise with simple walks through natural environments but also resting with power naps and a good night's sleep. What appears to be a waste of time actually allows you to be more focused.

Taking care of your mind allows you to be more open to the learning opportunities presented throughout life. It implies reading and listening but also sharing your thoughts and ideas.

Taking care of your spiritual path allows you to develop your creativity. Some persons believe in God, others in spiritual realities, and others believe in the human spirit alone. But I guess we all agree on realities beyond space and time, which we perceive through our consciousness and self-awareness. Learning often implies such inner processes to manifest themselves in life.

Taking care of your relationships allows you to live more fully. What are we without our relationships? Drifters in life. And someone drifting in life won't go anywhere or live without knowing where to go. Relationships allow us to ground our learning in life and not in our intellect alone. Relationships allow learning to become transformative, and that's what relational learning is all about.

CAUSING

How can your life inspire everyone to enjoy learning?

What makes someone an interesting person? Is it the number of things she knows? Does she have an intriguing personality? It could be. But I wonder if it could be the fact this person is a cause of learning.

Every person we feel we can learn something with every time we're together is an interesting person. People who are a cause of learning have certain traits. They're good listeners, don't speak but the essential, and bring joy with their presence. Moreover, they make you feel important to them and have the utmost respect for what you think and do. And because of their attentive mindset, the right word at the right time is a cause of learning for you.

The simplicity that transpired from their life is

attractive. The humble mindset when they share their creativity inspires them. You learn from them because they learn from you first and make sure you know it.

CHANCE

We change whenever we meet another person because we're constantly changed by the relationships we have. In this sense, every person is a novelty for you, even if you "think" you have known her for years.

As Learning Minds, we learn from everything and everyone every day. However, each person we meet is an inexhaustible source of novelty and, consequently, of learning.

Relationships are the best source for learning new things, like inspiring ideas from others, even if they are unaware of it.

One time, my daughter looked at me and said - "here we have heat, *and there we have cold.*" As a professor in Heat Transfer, I told her - "*you know, cold doesn't exist. It is the absence of heat.*" Then she welcomed what I said with - "*Oh! So, here, there's heat, and heat is absent. And if there's no heat, there's room for heat to enter."* Wow! I never thought about this perspective, but it's an accurate and visual way to explain what happens.

Cherish your relationships. They are the best chance you'll have of learning new things every day.

COHERENCE

We have the skill to learn something new every day, but how much does it transform our lives?

Being a learning mind implies opening our knowledge to the new experiences we live every day. And every new topic or thought, a new word or idea should produce an impact in our lives.

The challenge is to live according to this new learning. It takes time, mistakes, restarting, and keep learning. Only if we *keep learning* will we live coherently with what we learn.

COMPASS

ost people who don't realize how important learning is live as if mindlessly following their GPS. If the map is outdated, they fail to adapt and fail to reach their destination.

But if you have a map and a special compass that points to where you want to go, like in the movie Pirates of the Caribbean, you only need to follow the path.

The problem is knowing where you want to go.

People without goals live in a random magnetic field with the compass needle pointing nowhere. And people who don't yet know who they want to be have a lot of trouble setting goals in their lives. Therefore, it all comes down to your identity.

Take an hour, a day, a week, but think carefully about who you want to be. Afterward, it is easier to find the goals which allow you to get there. The miracle compass that points the way is your habits. And the map is the world, the birthplace of creativity, when we allow ourselves to be lifelong learners.

COURAGE

Fear may stop us from reaching our goals and dreams. And we think the best way to overcome fear is with courage. But let us use *learning* instead.

Modern fears include FOMO (Fear-Of-Missing-Out) and social media anxiety, but the greatest fear of all is the fear of failure. Failure in life, in our work, in our dreams and desires.

Every fear points to something we can learn to experience transformation, know more about who we are, and improve what we do.

If I fear failing at a conference presentation, it points to the value of learning to prepare it with time and dedication.

If I fear failing at a deadline for a project, it leads to the importance of learning to organize myself better and overcome procrastination.

If I fear failing someone's expectations, it points to learning to accept myself as I am and acknowledge that I can be better if I keep learning.

CONNECTION

*L*earning demands you to focus, and most people can concentrate when they're alone. Therefore, it's easier to isolate yourself while learning than you think. But is this isolation a good thing?

If you're online in a webinar or watching e-course videos, you're by yourself.

If you're learning in class, be it in a large or small group, and you sit silently and leave without a word, you're by yourself.

But if the words in a TED talk make you excited, and you feel you're learning, why is this different from the most typical forms of learning? No one usually feels excited about formal learning, which - unfortunately - relates more to learning in isolation than we would like.

Learning is about connection. You are connecting the dots. Connecting your experience with the experience of others and connecting in dialogue with your peers because you achieve the best learning when you make it a relational experience. But there's something you cannot neglect.

Even if learning is relational, it doesn't eliminate the fact that you have to do your part. Relational learning does not mean someone is going to learn for you. Quite the contrary, it counts on you to learn as well.

When we think we can learn alone, all by ourselves, it seems noble, but such independence means more isolation than autonomy, which is an essential trait in learning.

In autonomy, doing your part means developing the intellectual resources that contribute to the learning process. But you only know if you're autonomous when you confront what you learned with someone else. Otherwise, you may live an illusion. But how can growing your autonomy be compatible with relational learning?

When we foster autonomy, we feel compelled to share what we learn with others and help them find their way toward autonomy, too. This reciprocal autonomy generates connection and it is an essential part of what relational learning is all about.

CULTIVATE

We often use the word "heart" to mean everything we are and ever will be. It means the core of who we are. I believe learning should be at that core, which is why we should cultivate it.

The best way to cultivate learning in your heart is through experience. When we experience learning new things, we feel rewarded, not because of their usefulness.

True learning allows us to go beyond how we can use what we learn.

True learning humanizes us and how we view others and life. It will give us a Big Inner Transformative (BIT) vision of who we can be. We can accept who we are or cultivate learning in our hearts to discover who we can become.

Being is not at the heart of a learning mind. Becoming is.

CULTURE

*I*f learning is part of what biologically helped us survive and thrive as a species in the biosphere, learning is what culturally allowed us to grow in the noosphere. What is the noosphere?

Noosphere is the sphere of human thought, just as the biosphere is the sphere of life on this planet. The word has its roots in the Greek "*nous*" which means *mind,* and *sphaira* (sphere). Pierre Teilhard de Chardin, a paleontologist and Jesuit priest, introduced it to indicate the emergence of human cognition, which transforms the biosphere.

"And this amounts to imagining, in one way or another, above the animal biosphere a human sphere, a sphere of reflection, of conscious invention, of conscious souls (the noosphere, if you will)."

(P. Teilhard de Chardin)

Therefore, learning emerges when another form of evolution appears with our species, a cultural evolution. But is there a limit to what we can learn?

A few days ago, I found an awkward idea.

Learning is our superpower.

We don't need the super-power of flying, because we learn how to do it using what we learned and developing technology. The same goes for strength above our possibilities, long-distance communication, speed, sight, etc. Behind all our achievements is not only the human spirit but our ability to learn.

However, in the age of social media, I fear we allow ourselves to be grabbed by its attention drainage power in such a way that we stopped growing our ability to learn. We prefer to consume whatever information is available at our fingertips and be content.

Suppose we invest in growing a Culture of Learning by trying to learn something new every day and begin to love learning again. In that case, we will rediscover the possibilities opened by using our super-power. I sense what lies ahead if we follow this path is more significant than our imagination can muster.

CURATION

The amount of information available in this century is incommensurable. The primary challenge is to make sense of it.

In a museum, the several elements of a certain historical period are not exposed randomly but curated thoughtfully. In a way, the visitor feels immersed in a meaningful thread.

The same occurs with lifelong learning. As Jeff Cobb recently wrote[1]

"Curating for learning involves making choices about content and experiences from among a large number of options; infusing those choices with context and meaning; and sharing the results with others."

The job of a curator is to make sense of things in the world and, in the case of learning, make sense of the information available. Being a curator takes time and effort. Therefore, we don't need to aspire to be curators ourselves but find, and Jeff Cobb suggests, people who have done it for some time.

The question is: how do you choose?

People with ideas similar to yours run the risk of leading you to an echo chamber, or filter-bubble, where you don't learn much but keep confirming what you already think and know.

People with challenging ideas, even if you don't agree with them all the time, are the best to follow and interact with. In my case, I find Cal Newport to be one of such curators. But also Seth Godin, Jeff Cobb, Michael Hyatt, Simon Sinek, Jeff Goins, and others.

You may become a curator yourself.

It takes time, patience, attention, curiosity, resilience, humility and vulnerability. It takes lifelong learning, which we can start at any point in our lives because every age is right for learning.

DARE

It is not because things are difficult that we do not dare; it is because we do not dare that they are difficult. (Seneca)

Daring is a decision of the mind coherent with what you believe. If you believe you can learn anything, your mind is set, and even your body will follow.

A study published in Nature Human Behavior[1] suggests the mind affects your physiology more than you think.

If you wish to develop the super-power of learning and actively participate in the next step of human evolution, let me clarify it for you: dare to learn.

DECIDE

*I*s learning an option?

When you make it an option, a choice, it means you're free not to learn. But can you live without learning? You can, but you won't evolve. If you want to grow in your knowledge, skills, and personality, learning is the best, long-lasting way.

Learning is a decision toward making transformative experiences in your life. And the more you learn, the more you begin to love learning. And what endures in our lives is what we love.

Decide to learn today, every day. It can be a new word, a new instrument, a new idea, a new skill, a new meal, a new town, a new language, a new fact, or a new story. When you decide to learn, you choose what is new to you, and this will renew you every day.

DECLUTTER

*True detachment isn't a separation from life
but the absolute freedom within your mind
to explore living. (Ron Rathbun)*

Can we learn a simple way to live less stressfully? Declutter. That's it.

A study published in *Current Psychology*[1] found a correlation between a cluttered space and procrastination. As a side effect, your cortisol levels increase, which is the hormone related to stress.

Depending on your emotional state, decluttering your home or working space can be difficult. For extreme cases, experts recommend a hands-off approach and have someone do it for you. The reason is related to attachments to items you touch, making it hard to get rid of them and declutter.

However, the best approach might be minimalist. If you have less, there are fewer things to clutter your space, and the likelihood of living less stressfully increases.

But I think there is a less-known way that can help you learn how to declutter.

Detachment.

Decluttering as part of living detachment means an experience for deeper involvement with the way your life is taking. Therefore, if you practice detachment to experience greater freedom, my first suggestion is to start with your working table. Well, at least, that's what I often do.

DIFFERENT

The difficulty in learning is not getting things wrong, but if you stop because of it.

Although we live in a society expecting you to *Get Things Done*, if you don't master what others expect from you, the most common experience is to *Get Things Wrong*, and feel disappointed with yourself. It is not a problem as long as you have a growth mindset and keep improving your skills. But some people get tired of getting things wrong and stop. I get it.

Nobody likes getting things wrong over and over again. Logically, you feel - *"Maybe I should invest my time doing something else."* This decision is always a possibility. But don't you wonder what you can learn from mistakes?

If you stop at wrong, how can you expect to get it right? Learning implies you explore your limitations to understand the best way to overcome them.

Sometimes, the opposite of *wrong* is not *right*, but *different*. This is the perspective you get when you don't stop at wrong and keep learning. Eventually, you get things done, but differently. And that is often the genesis of innovation.

DIGNITY

The first step to promote peace in any region of the world devastated by war is making sure children go to school. Why? Because learning is the best survival skill we have in difficult times and more.

When we learn, we begin to evolve in our thinking and question how our actions can improve the world around us. We don't merely learn because it feels good, although it does. We learn to understand better the "why" affecting our world and society.

When we can provide a learning experience to every human being, we recognize their value as a person and their worthiness.

We dignify.

But there's another side of the story. Every person is a mystery to everyone else, which is why we can always learn something new by relating with another person. Learning is deeply relational, after all. Therefore, if we promote learning in others, we create learning opportunities for ourselves once we connect with them. Ultimately, we rediscover our worth as well as our dignity.

What dignifying learning opportunities can you create today?

DIVERSIFY

There are so many different things we can learn from our diversity.

Our differences divide us when we're blind to the richness in others. Different thoughts, ways of life, and cultures are natural. We understand this clearly if we contemplate nature and notice its biodiversity.

But we can see it also in larger urban areas where different people meet and build relationships.

If this is a reality of life, it should be no different for learning. One way to explore and develop our learnability is to diversify our learning. We'll discover more about ourselves than we think.

DOPAMINE

addiction affects learning, and I'm not referring to drugs, but a substance we produce in our brains. Dopamine.

Every coin has two different sides.

The negative side of dopamine is not working on our learning when we have the chance, like in a class, and opt to spend our attention on Facebook, texting or browsing. This addiction generates irreversibilities in the learning process, which demands a lot of effort to recover.

The positive side is to invest in learning one small thing at a time. Each time will release some dopamine from the sense of accomplishment. We may be so overwhelmed by actual learning that we keep producing dopamine, and learning can become addictive.

The negative side depletes our willpower and cognitive energy. The positive side does the opposite. Which one would you choose?

The second option, right? But what I experienced today with my students was otherwise, since they often opt for the first. At the end of class, I sincerely gave them my apologies because I failed to persuade them to pursue the positive side of dopamine.

It means I'm still learning and asking myself: what is the smallest thing I can do tomorrow to work on my persuasion skills?

DREAMING

Who doesn't want to fulfill his dreams? But where does the motivation to do anything to fulfill our dreams come from? A goal. A purpose. If you don't have one, difficulties arise, and you shift your path because, in reality, you don't know where to go.

Goals are important, and writing them on paper increases the probability of accomplishing them. But if you don't revisit what you write, you might forget.

Why do we keep procrastinating? That is the loss, even if only temporary, of our sense of "why." I've been reading a lot about productivity and better ways to accomplish my goals. I've been reading about the brain and body. About motivation and learning. I want to share all that is going through my mind in a new way. A compelling, exciting, and life-changing way.

Why?

Get authority on the matter? Write a book and be recognized? Earn more money?

Why?

Is the loss of our sense of why influencing our performance?

Are we tired of working intensely without end?

Would we like to be at a better stage of the things we wish to accomplish?

So, why do we keep procrastinating in the worst moments when a lot should be finished? I "still" don't know.

Maybe it is a question of motivation. Maybe it is a question of experiencing no reward and some feedback.

In my case, I write and share my thoughts with the world through the internet, but are people reading what I write? Yes, they are. One or two, occasionally. But am I getting feedback and stimulating discussion? No, I am not. So, what's the point?

This is resistance at its best, telling me to stop trying and procrastinate. I'm not giving up, and neither should you if you feel the same kind of resistance. It takes time and patience to fulfill our dreams. But the most important part is not fulfilling them but never ceases to dream.

EDUCATION

True education is a kind of never ending story
— a matter of continual beginnings, of
habitual fresh starts, of persistent newness.
(J.R.R. Tolkien)

Habitual learning is what you get when you learn something repeatedly until it becomes a habit. For example, my sister is a dentist and told me I had to floss my teeth. I didn't know how to do it properly, and the first time took quite a while. With time and practice, I made progress.

What if we made learning a habit? Practicing learning every day means educating ourselves with new things. New words, expressions, ideas, techniques. However, it implies recovering the real sense of education.

If you go to a dictionary, *education* means *"the process*

of receiving or giving systematic instruction," or it refers to the *"body of knowledge acquired."* But this is not the real sense of education. I fear we might be misled to think about education as instruction when it means a lot more.

Going to the etymology of the word, from the Latin *"educare,"* education means to bring up, to train. Still, there is also a version of its understanding pointing to something leading forth or bringing out. Something that changes from within where the mind and heart reside. It is the understanding of education as what unfolds the power of the mind.

Education, in its most profound sense, is the lifelong result of making learning a habit.

ENERGY

*Learning is movement from moment to
moment. (J. Krishnamurti)*

*E*nergeia is the Greek etymology for the word
energy, which means action—a word imbued
with dynamics and movement, much like learning.

People often think they learn by watching videos.
But they're mistaken. We may see Cristiano Ronaldo all
the time on the TV playing football, but it doesn't mean
we'll play like he does.

Learning is more than reasoning or thinking. It is an
experience. You need your mind, heart, and, especially,
your hands.

"We learn to do something by doing it. There is no other way." (John Holt)

Every movement only makes sense if you're doing something. Therefore, from the present moment to the next, there is a learning opportunity at your grasp. And what is this moving between moments if not life itself? If we become aware of this fact, we cannot live without learning or learn without living.

Living and learning are profoundly connected.

The energy of learning that flows is you.

ENTHUSIASM

*E*very time we learn with enthusiasm, our brain releases its dopamine neurotransmitters, which allow us to experience learning as rewarding and motivating.

The origin of the word *enthusiasm* means "possessed by God" or "divine inspiration," which translated to the learning context means experiencing a moment of creativity. When we experience learning as a creative moment in our lives, we feel enthusiastic and happy.

Therefore, learning with enthusiasm is the best road to long-lasting happiness. The challenge is boredom.

In many situations, the surroundings, the topic, or even the teacher or mentor is boring, and it isn't easy to feel any enthusiasm while learning. What can you do?

Use your imagination.

Imagine the boring teacher with a fruit hat on their head. Imagine anything that makes you smile with the topic boring you. Imagine different surroundings, like being immersed in nature or close to a waterfall.

There are no bounds to human imagination, but there is something that can supersede it.

" Life has more imagination than we carry in our dreams." (Christopher Columbus)

When we confront the most boring thing in our lives, we enter a different level of engagement because of the emotions associated with our experience. It's like when we were children and felt excited about the smallest ridiculous thing. With time, the system removed the genuity of the child within us and asked us to block our emotions through formalized learning.

It's time to break this barrier.

It's time to look at every learning opportunity through a child's eyes and begin learning with enthusiasm again.

EVOLVE

Since Darwin, we have thought about evolution as a competition for being the best, and the best survives. But what if you don't have enough resources to compete in the first place?

If you have fewer resources, you're more likely to collaborate with others. And from cooperation comes survival. This is why Peter Kropotkin found the same theory of evolution as Darwin but from a less resourceful and more cooperative point of view.

The ground for competition and cooperation are relationships. Therefore, relationships are the framework of evolution. If we want to evolve in anything we do - our work, our life - we need to care for our relationships.

In plentiful times, we compete. In scarcity, we cooperate. And I think the balance between competing and cooperating, regardless of resources, is focusing on the essentials.

In the essential, relationships thrive, and whatever you do and are evolves.

FAILING

Fail. Fail again. Fail better. (Samuel Beckett)

None of us always succeeds. We all fail at some point in something we try to learn anew. If we know this, we know we're not alone.

For people with a fixed mindset, failing once or more than once is a sign of not being able to succeed. They think being the best means always being the best. And by "best" they understand someone who does things right all the time. Nothing could be farther from the truth.

Everyone fails because it's the best way to learn and the right way.

Failing is nothing but exploring the chart of learnability.

The wrong way is not bad, but we can use the experience to understand better what we can change to move in the right direction. And the most important thing is knowing we're not alone when we fail.

FAITHFUL

The grand narrative of our life unfolds in how faithful we are to the small things. It is not easy, but we can learn. The question is: how?

There are several reasons why we may fail in small things, but in my experience, I see four: 1) forgetting, 2) bad habits, 3) distraction, and 4) negligence.

DON'T WAIT

The best way to avoid forgetting is to address the small things the moment they come up. You can use reminders apps, or write in a small pad the small things you need to remember. However, even with simple strategies, you may still forget. Addressing the second reason might help.

CREATE GOOD HABITS

By bad habits, I mean procrastination or too much switch-tasking (not multitasking because it's a myth), which distracts you from small things. The best way to overcome bad habits is to create new ones and good ones. And the best way to develop good habits is, precisely, through small things. They are so small you can't ignore them. There's an enormous reward feeling when you accomplish something, no matter how small.

PAY ATTENTION

If you want to remember and create good habits, you also need to pay attention. If we develop the skill of paying attention, it's easier to remember small things and take small actions that create good habits. If we survived as a species, it was mostly the result of paying attention.

VALUE SMALLNESS

Finally, we often neglect the small things and stop being faithful to them because we think they're unimportant. But consider how a small virus may affect your entire body and make you collapse, or an entire culture like we experienced with Covid-19. Consider how small is a tipping point, expressed as a moment in time, which turns your life around into something completely different. If you value smallness, incremental change happens, and you consolidate your life.

We may forget, fail, and disregard being faithful to the small things, but once we experience how much we learn by being faithful, we'll discover a more meaningful life. And who doesn't want that?

FIRST

Success is often measured by who arrived first, but those who fail are the first to learn. In the long run, they go farther.

Learning is not a matter of accepting you failed and trying again. It is a process of understanding why you failed, keep failing, but learn to fail better.

Before realizing the tremendous power of learning in my life, I thought success was amounting to small achievements, and it is. Still, every time I read success stories of people who changed the world, like Thomas Edison, I understand how their success included many failings. Not failures.

They show if you're always the first to learn, you're at the pole position of an enduring and rewarding successful life. To make sure of this, every time you fail, ask yourself - *"what can I learn?"*

The search prompted by the learning path is the way to perennial success, transforming your life and the lives of those around you.

FORGETTING

 s I read in an article[1] by Benedict Carey,

"To intentionally forget is to remember differently, on purpose."

The study he reported explained how we can refine our memory on purpose[2]. We have to recall and change it to improve. The authors concluded,

"To forget a memory, its mental representation should be enhanced to trigger memory weakening."

Thus, you have to strengthen your memory before weakening it. Counter-intuitive, no doubt.

You can suppress or substitute a memory, and this strategy of forgetting by changing that memory can be valuable when our life is affected by memories of trauma, shame, or neglect.

You're not changing what you lived, but making those memories that matter in your life. For example, remember the last time you felt humiliated. It's better to remember those who supported you than the humiliation.

FREE-FROM-FEAR

Fear is not a bad feeling when it helps to survive in harsh environments by making us alert. But fear may stop us from moving forward with our lives and becoming who we could be.

Learning is one of the most liberating experiences in life. It's our superpower. And like any super-power, the hero needs to spend time and effort and fail a lot before putting his abilities to good use.

The more we learn, the strongest we become in what we can do, and we keep on learning more and more. Eventually, fears either vanish or cease to stop us but instead serve as fuel to keep burning the light of learning.

Learning frees us from fear by making it useful to keep on learning.

GRATEFUL

*L*earning is rewarding when we experience the results firsthand. However, the reward feeling converts to gratefulness when we realize *learning* is a gift.

A gift is not something we possess but welcome. Learning is more than a skill or a trait. Learning is a way of being human, passed from generation to generation as a gift. In some parts of the world, learning is not easy or even possible—at least learning in its purest sense of curiosity. Where learning is difficult, the most basic learning is how to survive.

In developing countries, one of the first things missionaries and ONGs build besides hospitals is schools. It is consonant with learning as the superpower, allowing nations to thrive more than survive. In richer countries, we tend to oversee the opportunity every child has to learn with no worries about putting food on the table, having clothes to wear, and a warm house to shelter from the cold and rain.

We are not entitled to learning, but it is given to us by a society that knows its value in our growth as humans. Today, we should be grateful for the gift of learning and do everything in our power to ensure every human on this Earth can cherish this gift, too.

GROW

e cannot change skills but develop them. And we all have skills. But such development depends on our behavior. Therefore, to develop some skills, we need to change our behavior. We call developing and change growing.

Consider a college student. Anyone entering college can succeed. However, as a professional thinker, unless he develops the skill to think better, faster, and deeper, his success is not what it can be.

Behavioral choices are the greatest reason for a college student to under-develop his thinking skills. The decision of being constantly distracted with a smartphone or mere small talk instead of paying attention and thinking. He has the skill to think, but developing means choosing a mindful behavior and challenging what he learns.

This happens with any other skills you want to develop. And the best way to change your behavior is by clarifying who you are. And you are who you want to be. Keep that in mind and think.

INVOLVE

Education is what remains after one has
forgotten what one has learned in school.
(A. Einstein)

e can always learn by ourselves if we set our minds to it. But there's so much more we can learn if we get others involved and involve ourselves with others.

We can study with others. Develop with others new knowledge. We can share with others what we learn and ask for feedback. Ask others to teach us a craft. All this is because *learning is relational.*

Learning is an essential part of what makes us unique. As I read in Scientific American,

"Human accomplishments derive from our ability to acquire knowledge from others and to use that communal store of experience to devise novel solutions to life's challenges."

We may think that learning with others happens when we are at school, but education is something that lasts for a lifetime. Following Einstein, the best way to ensure education remains is to keep learning, and if we get others involved, it's more than rewarding. It's evolutionary.

JOYFUL

At the end of each year, we reflect on the past and everything we learned. Isn't the sentiment always joyful? What is learning for, if not to bring us joy?

At the beginning of 2018, I wanted to experience a LOL approach to learning—a Learn-Out-Loud inspired by what Tim Ferriss did with his life. I never thought of gradually discovering learning as one of our most significant sources of joy.

As a Professor, there is nothing more rewarding than seeing my students succeed. But when I began suggesting several tips to help them learn better, I looked at my life, and I wasn't a role model.

For more than ten years, I bragged about sleeping 5 hours per day - *"And look at how productive I am?"* But, between 2016 and 2017, I was tired, lost focus and began to decrease the quality of what I was producing.

Helping my students saved me, as I started to learn new ways of being more productive to teach them. At the end of 2018, I felt an enormous sense of joy.

Every time I learn something new, the feeling is always the same.

Joy.

When all over the world, the celebration of entering a New Year begins, remember how learning is always joyful.

I remember proposing once to my readers, to make the year 2019 the Year of Attention. Now you understand why.

With attention comes better learning.

And better learning gives you more joy.

KEY

Remember Einstein. His genius didn't come from knowing a lot but imagining simple things and having a curious and resilient mindset to pursue revolutionary ideas.

The key element is *imagination.*

How can we stimulate our imagination?

"The human mind is an incredible thing. It can conceive of the magnificence of the heavens and the intricacies of the basic components of matter. Yet for each mind to achieve its full potential, it needs a spark. The spark of inquiry and wonder." (Stephen Hawking)

We are so keen on usefulness, entertainment, swipe, and tapping that we risk losing track of a genuine fascination with the real world around us, replacing it with a virtual world. We need to find the right balance between both. How?

"Be curious. And however difficult life may seem, there is always something you can do and succeed at. It matters that you don't just give up. Unleash your imagination. Shape the future." (Stephen Hawking)

And keep learning every day, all the way. And one day, you'll discover the key phrase unlocking every learning experience - *"Hum, that's intriguing..."*

LAST

Zyzzyva. This is the last word in the English dictionary. But, what are words for, anyway? According to the Oxford Dictionary, Zyzzyva is

"a genus of tropical weevils (family *Curculionidae*) native to South America and typically found on or near palm trees. Also (in form zyzzyva): a weevil of this genus."

You know I'm Portuguese. Thus, when I read the definition of "Zyzzyva," I thought - *" what is weevil?"*
Weevil is

" From Middle English "wevel," from Old English "wifel" ("beetle"), said to be from the woven appearance of a weevil's larval case."

So, it's a beetle. Our unfamiliarity with words can send us on a path of discovering the world. Words are our way of expressing our understanding of reality, but there is something more profound than words and toward which words point.

" The language of friendship is not words but meanings." (Henry David Thoreau)

What are words for if devoid of *meaning*? It's like Stephen Robles says,

" The Internet has stolen some of our best words. "Spectacular", "Unbelievable", "Astonishing". These words used to be saved for those truly awe-inspiring moments. Now they are just cheap tricks to make a headline more appealing."

It's essential to choose words wisely.

" Whatever words we utter should be chosen with care for people will hear them and be influenced by them for good or ill." (Buddha)

If words shape our world, our reality, and the way we live it, maybe we should respect words more to learn how we can respect reality better, especially the people who live in it.

LEAP

What is a learning leap? A decision? A step in your learning path? The need to overcome obstacles or abysses? No. It is the unexpected leap of *showing up.*

People expect that learning is affected by your degree of attention, the amount of curiosity, whether you're resilient when you fail, or even humble enough to recognize the need to keep learning. People rarely expect the vulnerable side of learning.

A vulnerable mindset helps you take the learning leap to a new and deeper level. When you expose yourself and show up, allowing others to see your limitations, you are braver than you think.

"Embracing our vulnerabilities is risky but not nearly as dangerous as giving up on love and belonging and joy—the experiences that make us the most vulnerable.

Only when we are brave enough to explore the darkness will we discover the infinite power of our light." (Brené Brown)

The experience of learning makes you vulnerable because it is one of love, belonging, and joy. But it will transform your life forever. Embracing your vulnerability is the learning leap few people expect and there's no better way to surprise yourself and others than taking it.

LIFELONG

*L*earning every day is something you can do. But can we remember at the end of every day what new things we learned? It's not easy. We may even wonder if lifelong learning is a reality for us. I read from Seth Godin the following insight.

"Lifelong learning is the mindset of possibility. It is built on the idea that we can grow if we simply show up, ready to learn.

Lifelong learning is never finished, and achieving the mindset isn't easy, because the existing bias toward competence makes it socially unattractive. It requires us to acknowledge that we don't know enough on our way to learning more."

However, if we, as learning minds, develop a humble mindset, acknowledging we don't know enough is a testimony of having an open mind. Open-minded people allow an easier flow of learning and recognize mistakes as part of their evolutionary path.

Sometimes, an open mind is an emptied mind. We strive to give mental space to the new. It isn't easy, and that is the reason why lifelong learning becomes more than a possibility when we experience it as a daily reality.

Remember, it is a worthy step, even if it takes a lifetime to learn.

LISTENING

There's a lot of difference between listening and hearing. (G.K. Chesterton)

nd the difference is whether you pay your entire attention to the other person or not.

When you listen deeply to someone, there's no one else in the world but the person you listen to. Also, when you listen, you feel interested in what the other person is saying, and you try to understand her.

Listening is much more than being quiet. It is attending to a basic human need of the other, like water or food. The need for attention. You understand this need if you think about the times you needed someone to listen to you and remember what you were living.

If you master the listening skill, you'll likely master your learnability and create the bonds enhancing relational learning. Mastering the art of listening implies six simple choices.

EYE CONTACT

When you look in the eyes of the person teaching, you enhance the comprehension of what they are saying but also memorize better that moment. The eye contact shows how much you care for the other and your learning.

SILENT

The letters in the words *listen* and *silent* are the same because both are intrinsically related.

> "We have two ears and only one tongue so that we may hear more and speak less." (Diogenes Laertius)

QUESTION

There are two purposes for interrupting someone in a conversation: say something or ask for something. While the first means you haven't emptied your thoughts to listen actively, the second is the result of listening and searching for a better understanding.

You ask questions to clarify, go deeper into what the other is saying, and enter into the heart of listening and learning through listening flows through questions.

EMPTINESS

Forming responses in your mind while listening to someone is a form of cluttering the space of understanding. The art of listening requires space to connect the dots between the newly received information and your experience. You can do it by emptying your thoughts.

GESTURES

The art of listening moves your body toward gestures expressing non-verbal communication, affecting the interaction with the person from whom you're learning. If your gestures welcome what the other is saying, your body shows you are listening. The other feels motivated to transmit the message, and the result is improved learning.

OBSERVE

When you listen to learn, you observe. Attentive eyes are a sign of active listening, and the chances of memorizing what you are learning increase dramatically.

· · ·

IT'S NEVER TOO late to become an artist of listening. Cultivate a learning mind, be happier, and evolve. Don't start one day. Choose day one and start.

MAXIMIZE

I saw an infographic with a synthesis of 12 ways to maximize the way we think.[1] Guess one.

LEARNING HOW TO LEARN.

This maximization of the way you think involves developing your working memory, deliberate practice, time-chunking your activities, questioning and being curious, and overcoming the forgetting curve with spaced learning and time.

When you develop the skill of learning how to learn, you increase exponentially the number of things learned per hour. But you also learn better, and this allows you to adapt to any working environment faster than others. But there's a catch.

Alone, we may reach our goals faster, but together, we go farther. The most significant value in learning how to learn is in teaching it to others because learning is profoundly relational.

MESSENGERS

*O*nce we recognize ourselves as learning minds, the best way to spread the word is by being the word. The messenger becomes the message.

A learning mind pays *attention* to its surroundings and the life experienced every minute.

It is *curious* about intriguing questions and searches for clues to follow a path of discovery.

In this path, a learning mind finds failure, but it is *resilient* and learns from mistakes.

However, regardless of the path and depth of her wisdom, a learning mind is *humble* and recognizes there is still so much she can learn.

Finally, she shows up and shares what she has learned, thus conveying the message experienced because she became sufficiently *vulnerable* to become the message.

The outcome of our message is one... *joy.*

MINDSET

It is more or less taken for granted that mind affects the body, although the pathways are still unknown. (Ellen Langer)

Once, a friend said - " I'm too old to learn a new computer language." - was she right?

A body growing old is evident, even if people paint their hair to avoid showing it and use skin creams to disguise their wrinkles. Also, people strive to keep their minds young. However, people might think being younger in the mind often means accepting modernity and thinking like young people, which is not what keeps your mind young.

We think taking care of the body influences the

mind, but we often forget how taking care of the mind influences your body more than you think.

In 2007, Alia Crum and Ellen Langer experimented on 84 women room attending in hotels[1]. All of them felt their poor physical condition was due to the lack of exercise. However, in one group, Crum and Langer informed how their work was good exercise and satisfied the Surgeon General's recommendations for an active lifestyle. The result was, compared to the control group, a decrease in weight, blood pressure, body fat, waist-to-hip ratio, and body mass index. All they needed was a *change in mindset* and a different thought to influence their body health.

The same goes for learning. We may feel that age is inadequate for learning new skills, but that is not the problem. Instead, it is the thought of not being able to learn because it is something reserved for a certain period of our younger lives.

Nothing could be farther from the experience. It only requires we change our mindset to that of a learning mind, which has no age. Giving an excuse for not learning a new skill due to your age is likely to be related to the fear of failing, which is something reserved for younger people. On the contrary, if age is proportional to wisdom, it should be easier to recognize your mistakes and move on.

We are never too old to change our mindset and become life-long learners. Being a learning mind is not a wish but a choice, and so is changing mindsets.

MOTIVATION

It is easy to feel motivated to learn the things you like. But what about the things you dislike?

In a recent article in Harvard Business Review, Elizabeth Saunders deals with this problem in a wider scope[1]. She proposes two steps that I find useful for learning.

The first step is to find a meaningful *WHY*. Finding the reasons *why* you learn or do anything at all is of paramount importance these days. People often complain about not having time to learn the things they need to, and I think where there's a reason, there's time. It's all about knowing why you learn the things you do, whether you like them or not.

The second step is about the strategy you use to learn regardless of how you feel. In this step, you have a personal and a relational approach.

The relational approach is to embrace the learning process as something you do with others and establish positive relationships or something you share with others to foster your relationships. The cue is making the learning of things you dislike a reason to deepen the relationships you like.

The personal approach has two parts. The first is to *simplify*. The simpler the task you need to perform while learning, the higher the likelihood of overcoming the lack of motivation. The second part is to *add something you like* to the learning you dislike. For example, you need to study a subject you don't like. Do it in a comfortable place where you feel concentrated. I remember experiencing this technique with an old couch I had in my bedroom and liked, and it worked.

The lack of motivation will always be part of lifelong learning. If you develop these two steps with creativity, you begin to gain the experience to overcome this obstacle.

MYSTERY

" Until we accept the fact that life itself is founded in mystery, we shall learn nothing." (Henry Miller)

Mysteries are hidden realities. Enigmas are problems we can solve, but I would distinguish them from mysteries. Solving a mystery is finding the hidden reality and uncovering new questions leading to new hidden realities and, thus, mysteries.

When we accept life is grounded in mystery, we welcome the hidden reality of life as an abundant source of surprise and imagination.

The course we set ourselves to uncover a mystery has more profound implications than we think. While we wonder if the endgame of immersing ourselves in solving a mystery is finding the hidden reality, I think the real purpose is living the path, the process.

We learn so much in processes that, eventually, mysteries are not meant to inspire us to solve the puzzle of reality and our lives. Mysteries can be one of the best ways to develop our ability to learn.

OPPORTUNITY

What if you made of your relationships learning opportunities? Taking care of another person's learning, besides developing your learnabilities, starts by taking care of your relationship with the other.

You may wonder if taking care of the learning of another person is making sure they study or you teach them something. But it is not.

The best way of caring for how others learn is to make yourself interesting and open enough so others feel the love of learning from you or are motivated by your relationship with you. And from that experience inspire them to learn for themselves.

Learning can be one of the most rewarding experiences in our lives. Caring for the other's learning, leads us to care for how we learn as well. An attentive and curious person is always eager to learn and, through the art of listening, inspires others to be more attentive and curious as well.

"You cannot open a book without learning something." (Confucius)

Be the book others can open to give them the opportunity to learn something when they read you.

OVERCOMING

earning is as hard as rewarding. And the most natural experience is the difficulty of learning. How can we overcome difficulties in learning?

When facing difficulties, we can overcome them in different ways.

We can *ignore* difficulties and "hope" for the best. This is the passive mindset of those who are slow learners.

We can *stop* at difficulties and give up learning. It's not for us. Sometimes, it might be a wise decision because there's no point in spending time learning what is not for us when we could use the time to learn other things more consonant with our life's present moment.

But, we can *study* difficulties and become experts in our failings. Failing is often the best teacher we have in life. And every setback can be an opportunity for learning. This resilient mindset is what allows overcoming difficulties by making them precious learning tools.

95

ing. This resilient mindset is what allows overcoming difficulties by making them precious learning tools.

PEACEMAKERS

Peace cannot be kept by force; it can only be achieved by understanding.
(Albert Einstein)

On the first day of a new year, we often experience peace and a fresh start. Without realizing it, learning can make you a peacemaker.

In conflicted areas, schools reopening is the first sign of peace. Since 2012, UNICEF has developed a Learning for Peace program "to strengthen resilience, social cohesion, and human security in conflict-affected contexts, including countries at risk of *experiencing or recovering from conflict. In particular, the Learning for Peace program aims at strengthening policies and practices in education for peacebuilding."*

More than resolving conflicts, learning provides the ground for mutual respect and a healthy relational environment. In small African villages where this program unrolls, the fact parents from different ethnic groups see their children playing with each other allows them to speak with each other. These are the first steps to peace.

"If you want to end the war (...) instead of sending guns, send books. Instead of sending tanks, send pens. Instead of sending soldiers, send teachers." (Malala Yousafzai, 17-year-old Noble Peace Laureate)

Learning is the relational framework, making each person a peacemaker. The more we invest in our learnability, the better we are at peacemaking.

The first day of every new year is the World Day of Peace. It is worth taking the first step to a new evolutionary chain of events. One which leads to a long-lasting peace. I believe this first step is simple: invest in your daily learning. Therefore, ask yourself - *"what can I learn today?"* - and keep asking every day.

Love is so short, forgetting is so long.
(Pablo Neruda)

Love is a high-attention phase in our lives, and once love fades, it also has memories. However, when we experience love as transformative, and such transformation endures throughout generations, forgetting becomes a slow process.

Inspired by Neruda's sentence, a group of researchers led by Christian Candia and César Hidalgo suggested that forgetting in our society follows a universal mathematical function with two memory components: communicative and cultural[1].

Communicative memory is the "Love is so short" part.

We pay a lot of attention at the beginning but easily forget after a short time. We associate this memory component with oral communication.

Cultural memory is the "forgetting is so long" which lasts as an intrinsic part of our human way of life since we physically record the information, thus, sustaining it for future generations.

The implications for learning are profound.

The first stage of learning is through oral communication, although in the digital age, social networking has extended the ways we communicate. But, even if the information is now digitally recorded, it doesn't mean we won't forget it. The pace at which we produce information can quickly turn something important irrelevant.

Only if we convert what we learn into part of our culture will such learning last. We see this in many teachings of the Stoics and the Prophets in the Bible, which produce an impact even today. And I would extend to everything we learn on a daily basis.

The challenge to a *learning mind* is the conversion of daily learning into cultural change. It isn't enough to communicate to others what we learn. Learning can only transform our lives if it changes how we do things and how we live. It means cultural change is significantly affected by what we learn every day.

There must be a moment when there is a transition between a high attention learning (communicative memory) into a cultural change that performs a life transformative experience (cultural memory). I call this moment the *Perennial Act: making what we learn into how we live.*

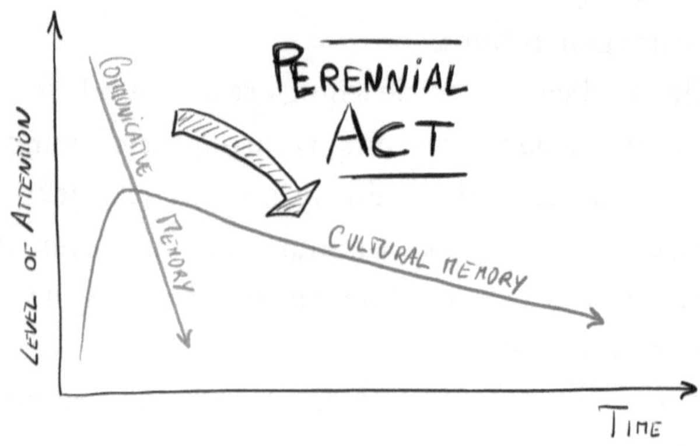

PERSUASIVE

*The best way to persuade others is with your
ears, by listening. (Dean Rusk)*

To the transition between a high attention learning (communicative memory) and a cultural change that performs a life-transformative experience (cultural memory), I called the *Perennial Act: making what we learn into how we live.* But, unless I'm able to persuade others of the possibilities opened by this act, it won't be perennial at all.

Persuasion comes from the ability to listen with an attentive mindset. When you listen with an open mind and heart, you decrease the resistance in the other because of the experience he makes of being heard.

Our intense digital lives give the impression that you're being heard, but it is an impression, not reality.

The reality is a massive sharing with the void, where the information flow defined by an algorithm decides what others hear from you.

Listening is an analog event that requires presence and bodily expression. In the end, we get *the persuasive act: inducing life-transformative change through attentive listening.*

POSSIBILITY

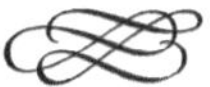

*E*very time we think about how hard learning is, we tend to forget the possibility such learning opens to us.

"Sometimes you win, sometimes you learn," says the title of John C. Maxwell's book. This means we never lose but learn. It requires a mindset change, detaching us from outcomes and focusing on processes.

We understand the implications of evolution by the outcomes, but every one of them is the result of a process.

If we set our minds on cherishing every process experienced in our lives, every event becomes a learning opportunity and opens our minds, hearts, and hands to new possibilities.

POWER

Knowledge is not power. Learning is. The power comes from a free mind, not money or the control of others. When you allow your learning mind to develop, you are free to think, create, and connect.

We live in the age of information with excessive flows around the world. It even gives us the feeling of unlimited access to knowledge. Thus, people may be deceived into thinking that knowing something empowers them. But this is not so.

We create knowledge by learning and understanding the world around us. And the more we seem to know, the better we realize there is so much we don't know. We only need an open learning mind to follow the path of the adventure of ideas.

Learn to learn better because that is where the power of a genuinely free mind flourishes.

PRESENT

So few people are really aware of their thoughts. Their minds run all over the place without their permission, and they go along for the ride unknowingly and without making a choice. (Thomas Sterner)

The past is gone. The future is yet to come. All you have is the present. The present moment is the best one to learn something worth living.

We learn with the past, although it's gone.

We learn with the perspective the future gives.

But understanding the past to set the course for a better future depends on what we learn in the present, and every moment counts.

Several studies point, on average, that we have

between 17 to 35 thoughts per minute. We're always thinking. And from the 25000 to 50000 thoughts we have per day, everything indicates a majority of 70% are negative thoughts. No wonder how important learning is, in the present moment, for the simple reason of generating more positive thoughts.

Learning builds skills and creates cultural change, but we shouldn't forget it affects our physiology, namely, our brain. Learning affects your body at every present moment.

When we learn something new, we create new neural pathways to connect the information acquired with prior knowledge. And the more connections we make, the higher the number of synapses in our brain. Our thoughts release chemicals that produce an impact on our body and how we feel. For example, positive thoughts decrease the levels of cortisol associated with stress and increase the levels of serotonin, associated with a sense of pride and confidence. We can focus more and become emotionally more stable. Positive thoughts also release dopamine, which is a well-known neurotransmitter of a sense of reward and pleasure. All this bodily experience happens when we learn in the present moment.

But... (there's always a "but"), what if you don't enjoy learning?

In this case, learning in the present moment would become the opposite of everything stated above. I want to challenge this impression. It is a matter of mindset and metacognition. And you can change it if you want.

You might not see any point in learning, and you can interpret the very thought of learning something as a negative experience. It follows an anxious, angry, disappointed, depressive state. If learning in the present moment requires new action every moment, you need to change the mindset to change the action to make learning a positive experience.

If you're unaware of the positive impact learning has in your life, giving more time to metacognition allows you to recover a learning awareness.

From my experience, since I began creating the habit of learning something new every day and sharing it with friends as a self-accountability strategy, my awareness of thought processes while learning has increased. Moreover, I began craving more learning, not more knowledge, because learning in the present moment means transforming information into knowledge and, through understanding what you know anew, translating it into life.

When learning in the present moment becomes life, that's the transformative moment that brings you to greater awareness, not of who you are, but more of who you may become.

RESTARTING

It's easy to feel boredom. You only need to stop learning. The problem is spending years or months without learning anything new until it becomes a habit.

Instead of welcoming new ways of thinking or doing things, you're content with the old and established. But what seems a comfortable way of life is incompatible with the narrative of the world. The pace is fast, and some things may change overnight. And the price you pay for ceasing to learn is sadness.

Not a sadness for the things you have and who you are because people are content. No. Sadness when you discover the things you could have done and the person you could have been and realize time hasn't stopped. If you feel this way, there's a solution.

Learning has no age.

As long as you're human, you have the inherent ability to learn. And when you begin to learn again, the outcome is more than acquiring new knowledge or skills. It is joy. Thus, if you want more joy in your life, the best way is to start to learn again.

RESPECT

Learning itself is universal, but the methods or the contents may differ. Respect is part of the humble mindset allowing us to welcome those who learn differently from us. It is a path with three insightful steps.

The first step to respect differences in learning is to recognize the value of other learning approaches. Such recognition doesn't require agreement, but if you understand how others have learned, you comprehend better their decisions and actions respectfully.

The second step is to approach other's learning experiences with empathy and constructively. Differences only divide in the absence of respect. When people respect each other, differences are a way of mutual enrichment.

The third step is to contrast different ways of

learning similar things creatively. True innovation often emerges from this contrast. But we need intellectual openness and a humble mindset to recognize the novelty inside differences.

RESTORE

The attention restoration theory explains how walking through nature can have a positive effect on your ability to focus.

Today, I did just that with my family in Luso (Portugal). More than living an adventure, we experience it together.

When was the last time you took your family to restore your attention?

Attention to each other.

Each fear.

Each joy.

Each obstacle.

The focus restored by nature ends up being the focus on the most meaningful choices in your life.

RIGHTEOUSNESS

If you would convince a man that he does
wrong, do right. But do not care to convince
him. Men will believe what they see. Let
them see. (Henry David Thoreau)

What if we learn something without realizing the purpose is hurting or manipulating other people?

What is righteous builds a united humanity. Thus, how can we know if anything we learn is righteous?

In my experience, the metric is simple. What is righteous builds free and enduring relationships.

All *relational learning* is righteous.

Relational learning is more than knowledge or even

applied knowledge. It is a life experience that generates positive, liberating, and transformative experiences in others.

SAKE

We should learn for the sake of learning. Any other reason seems worthless.

I got this impression from Csikszentmihalyi's book on *Creativity*. At a certain point, he says,

> "The many years of tedious calculations are vindicated by the burst of new knowledge. But even without success, creative persons find joy in a job well done. *Learning for its own sake is rewarding* [emphasis added] even if it fails to result in a public discovery."

Every minute we spend learning something new has its taste of success. We often give enormous value to the usefulness of what we learn, which becomes an impediment to learning.

If we *learn for its own sake*, the very act is rewarding enough, but it implies a mindset change. We do not learn because it's useful. We learn because we can. It's embedded in our humanity.

The next time you have an opportunity to learn, don't waste it. And if you think learning is tedious, good, in time, you'll understand it was never about the content but all about the process.

SEARCHING

Puzzles are more than a game. They're a source of daily learning.

With the excess of information at our reach, we experience a similar feeling as we look through all the pieces of a puzzle.

Suppose we have no idea what to search. It will take forever to put the pieces together.

Making a puzzle means searching for similar patterns and - with a bit of luck - finding the right piece at the right time.

What I've learned today is the importance of having an idea of what you're searching for. Otherwise, you experience a drifted search and a mindless life.

Knowing which piece you should look at is as simple as paying attention to details.

SLEEPING

"I'll sleep on it" might be truer than you think. The neuroscientist Michael Merzenich explains how sleep cleans irrelevant information during REM, consolidates information (moderate sleep), and chemically rejuvenates the brain.

An article[1] in the Wall Street Journal reported that some researchers believe sleep is a time to learn something new.

Hypnopedia is the term for sleep learning. The mechanism is the activation of the hippocampus (the area of the brain related to memory and learning) during certain sleep cycles. According to Dr. Sanam Hafeez, this activation happens through neural oscillations, or what we experience as up-and-down wakefulness when our heart slows and our body temperature drops. It is the consolidating phase Dr. Merzenich speaks about.

To take advantage of this, we are recommended to

cut coffee by 4 pm and exercise before going to bed. Not everyone endorses the last recommendation because people tend to eat after exercising, which is not good before going to sleep.

For many years, I didn't pay any attention to sleep and thought only unproductive people invested in sleeping. It was one of the biggest mistakes in my life and I see my students often repeat it. Students who study late before an exam and do it systematically throughout the week jeopardize their performance.

I recovered, but it took me more than a year. However, it's comforting to know research confirms any investment you make to improve how you sleep is worth the time. It will boost learning and this is music to the ears of any learning mind.

SOCIALIZE

There is an interesting remark by computer scientist and productivity expert Cal Newport about *Analog Social Media*. He describes it as " *organizations, activities, and traditions that require you to interact with interesting people and encounter interesting things in the real world.*" Joining this initiative means re-learning how to socialize.

Learners are fascinating people. They are attentive to everything everyone says. They respect the time to listen and be silent (remember it as the same letters as *listen*, only in a different order). They are humble in their views and always willing to show up and be there when you need them.

Re-learning to socialize means you have to move, take action, and look with your eyes fixed on others. While digital social media controls your eyes and what you see, analog social media leads you to experience better self-control of your eyes and attention.

To involve yourself in analog social media, you have to get out of your comfort zone, and that is the best attitude for learning.

In digital social media, you may try to spread an idea, but it is through analog social media that you make it happen in a transformative way.

Every social media reality has its place. The problem is when you replace one for the other. We may think our need to re-learn how to socialize means the recognition that humanity took a step backward in our cultural evolution. But I don't think so. Now, more than ever, we have the opportunity to find the rightful place of things undervalued in the past and use them to grow the learning capital that ensures a brighter future.

SOLIDARITY

Do you believe cold exists? It doesn't. It's the absence of heat. And according to my youngest - "if there's room, heat will go there." However, this shows me something deeply embedded in nature. Solidarity.

I understood this when I was teaching a class on heat conduction, where the mechanism through which heat flows in a material is by molecular diffusion.

We know a particle has more energy when its temperature is higher. Therefore, if it has energy, and next to it, there's a particle with less energy, it will "give" some of its energy to it. I realize this is an image of solidarity in nature.

Living with the essentials means having only what we need. If we have more than we need, the natural logic of gift should compel us to share with those who need more.

The reason for solidarity in nature is the dynamics associated with equilibriums. Why aren't we naturally inclined to live always in solidarity? Some think about the selfish nature of our genes, which inspires our memes. But I think it might be something else much more subtle.

Fear.

As long as we live attached to what we think we have and are entitled to, we understand the natural inclination for giving as losing. Instead of seeing a gift, we see a loss.

When we learn solidarity with nature, we'll experience a powerful feeling from the act of giving. Joy.

SPARK

Curiosity is the spark leading to insightful discoveries about the nature of reality which may produce an impact in our lives. Consider grapes.

An article in the New York Times by James Gorman synthesized the research of plasmas generated by grapes in a microwave[1]—a fun fact shared by many people online.

This online sharing led to innovative research on the propagation and concentration of microwaves inside a grape in a way never seen before.

But if scientists weren't paying attention, they might never see the connection. Attention is one of curiosity's main drivers.

Cultivate attention by thinking about things you see and let your curious mindset explore the possibilities opened by what you can learn.

SPIRITUAL

Think about three essential words for learning: *meaning, purpose, and connection.*

In an article[1], Vachel Miller, a professor at Appalachian State University, stated

"Spirituality has many definitions. For some, spirituality is a search for meaning, a desire to understand our lives in relation to Ultimate Being. It is, in the words of Catholic theologian David Steindl-Rast (1991), 'an insight through which our restless search finds rest.' For others, spirituality is a quest for self-transcendence, an encounter with mystery, or a feeling of universal interconnection. Spirituality can also be seen as attention to the divine presence in each other and in all aspects of daily life. In this discussion, the many connotations of spirituality will be compressed into three words: meaning, purpose, and connection."

The *search for meaning* is an intrinsic motivation driving every learning experience. Otherwise, why learn at all? We have unparalleled access to a considerable amount of information and knowledge. However, we feel restless until we fulfill the human need to make sense of all the knowledge available with our experiences, informing our identity.

The *search for purpose* is intrinsic to our desire to change as part of our timeless evolutionary drive. We do not rely on being as much as we rely on becoming because we crave personal growth, and learning fulfills that craving. Purpose is the source of our motivation for action toward deep learning about our place in the world and how to interact with it. As V. Miller says, *"purpose shapes what we pay attention to and what we work toward."* When our learning finds no purpose or serves the purpose of others, we resist. We need the space to define and pursue our goal to engage in learning.

The *search for connection* is embedded in our biological and cultural DNA. We are all interconnected, which is something present in all significant religious experiences through the Golden Rule, *"Do unto others as you would have them do unto you."* The world is not a mechanical clock that we can manipulate and fix when it is broken. When Darwin saw the machinery of life involved in evolution, the most appropriate expression would be the *web of life* because the world and our experiences in it are a dynamic reality of complex and everlasting relationships that evolve in depth. Learning is deeply related to human connection. We evolved through learning with other people, not in isolation, and through our relationships with the world around us. The search for connection is the reason why learning is more relational than rational. We form communities to make learning a relational and enriching experience. Even if every person has to do their part, we practice together what we learn. The greatest evidence in our digital age is the proliferation of communities of all sorts throughout the world using the internet. There-fore, it is essential to connect spirituality and learning to rediscover the evolutionary power of a learning society.

I agree with V. Miller when he says, *"in a learning society, we realize that spiritual concerns are learning concerns"* because spirituality reaches the most profound human aspirations about the search for meaning, purpose, and connection, which separated from the learning process would reduce to the accumulation of data, tasks and isolated moments in front of screens.

STOP

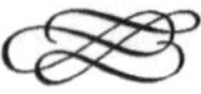

If you don't learn to stop, your body may break and then you stop learning.

Learning to stop is a skill.

Take a break.

Rest for a while.

Recover your strength.

STRIVING

Always remember that striving and struggle
precede success, even in the dictionary.
(Sarah Ban Breathnach)

Learning is much more than something you receive at school or even in life. It is the result of a striving experience that lasts your entire life. And those who strive for learning find it rewarding.

But, as Sarah Ban Breathnach says, striving precedes struggle before reaching success. And when we struggle, the likelihood of failing is high. It is good that failing is not the same as failure. Only those who never fail are a failure. However, even failing when we struggle to learn can have a different point of view.

"I have not failed. I've just found 10,000 ways that won't work." (Thomas A. Edison)

When we fail while striving for learning, it is more *waiting* than a struggle. I remember a sentence from Disney's Gyro Gearloose in front of my desk during my Ph.D. that said - *"I invent everything. The impossible only takes longer."*

In a world where people are getting used to having what they want, easy and fast, we gradually lose the value and power of waiting.

Keep striving.

Keep failing.

Wait.

And in time, you'll succeed.

STUDYING

What's the difference between learning and studying? We understand learning as gaining knowledge or a skill. And we do that through studying. Therefore, studying is one of the processes we can use while learning. Common sense says studying is one way to learn. But we still feel the gap when we study and don't learn. What possibilities open if we find a way to overcome this gap?

When we think about studying, we have in mind something we have to do. It is an obligation, not a choice, like in learning.

Also, we think of learning as the outcome of how much we study, but we often forget things after reaching the goal of studying in the first place (an exam, a presentation, etc.).

I wonder what could help to connect studying to learning.

From a curious mindset comes the fascination for whatever we learn, and from a resilient mindset comes the will to embrace the deliberate practice of studying.

But it is the feeling of *joy* when we are able to learn something after studying that provides an unforgettable experience.

The *joy of learning from a resilient curiosity* might unite learning and study in such a way they seem the same. Or better, we might realize they *were* the same all along.

SUPERPOWER

Undoubtedly, we become what we envisage.
(Claude M. Bristol)

e are what we experience, but what defines who we should become? And what matters most: being or becoming?

We may accept who we are and focus our lives on a fixed idea of ourselves. Albeit the importance of such self-acceptance, as learning minds, we are constantly changing. This change points to our becoming. How can we orient ourselves in becoming?

Unless we learn to see the big picture about ourselves, we may drift through life without becoming who we could be.

A humble mindset allows recognizing who we are

because it is the starting point of every journey into becoming who we can be. But unless we envision and dream ourselves ahead, we may lose the *way* because we are unaware of our *why*.

The simple exercise of imagining yourself in ten years is insightful. And even if the path changes due to circumstances, we welcome the unexpected and let it shape our becoming.

But I wonder if there is a universal idea of becoming that manifests in infinite tones throughout human history. I can think of one, and I believe it is our true superpower.

The power of learning awareness.

Learning is an everyday fact. But being aware of what we learn is not. And our becoming depends on how much awareness we have of what we learn every day.

A simple exercise for bringing greater awareness is to write in your journal something new you learned every day: a word, a fact, an idea, a name, anything. In time, it will unlock your learning superpower and who knows who you'll become and the kind of evolutionary path your life will bring to humanity.

TOUCH

*Touch is a reciprocal action, a gesture of
exchange with the world.*
(Robert MacFarlane)

When I began school, I was so excited about learning new things that as soon as I arrived home, I started teaching my younger sister what I learned. As soon as she started school, I noticed she was much better than I, and I'm happy to think I might have something to do with it.

When we were older, every time she asked for my help with something, I began explaining every detail, and she became tired, saying -" *I just asked you about this angle, not for the entire explanation of trigonometry!*"

Now that I'm a professor when my students talk to

each other during class and lack the motivation to pay attention, I feel sad because I realize the enormous learning potential being wasted right there in front of me. I warned them but wondered, have I lost the touch of making others learn better what I learned?

That's when it hit me. *Touch.*

Touching others must be an essential element of every learning process. It's the manifestation of inspiring moments.

Touching the mind and heart of a person is a delicate balance between excitement and observation, and learning this skill is a life-long process. Excitement shows how much you care about what you say. Observation gives you the necessary feedback to adjust how you're touching others.

When we think we lost *touch* maybe it means something else. Perhaps the art of touching others through our teaching, learning, and life experience evolves. How? I'm going to invest in being better at *making myself one* with those I mean to touch and see what happens.

TRANQUILITY

What do you want to learn today? Something mind-blowing? Something intriguing? Something unexpected? How about all three in one word: *tranquility*.

In *tranquility*, you'll find the time for the mind-blowing thoughts your chores don't allow.

In *tranquility*, you'll find the intriguing questions driving us toward the mystery every day offers.

In *tranquility*, you'll find the answers you least expect. Be surprised and find happiness.

Tranquility is one of those moments you will experience how blessed you are for being, naturally, alive.

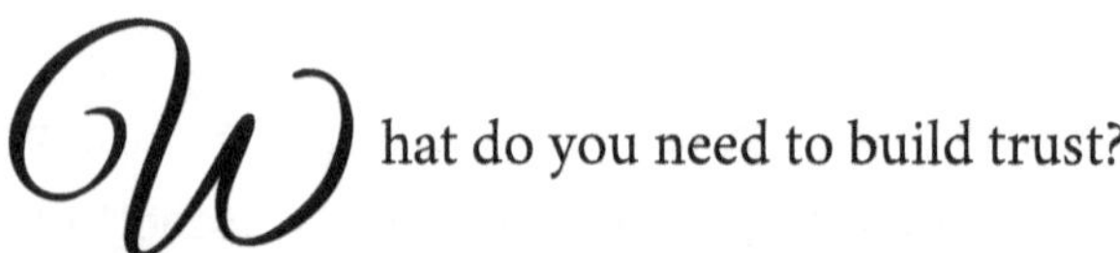

hat do you need to build trust?

I REMEMBER READING an article in Psychology Today pointing to five strategies:

1. generosity
2. patience and flexibility
3. reliability
4. consistency
5. openness

Learning means giving yourself to what you learn, and it requires a generous heart.

Learning means being patient toward your failings and flexibility to overcome challenges.

Learning means relying on others, as others rely on your dedication to the process.

Learning means being consistent and showing up every time.

Learning opens your mind to new possibilities and keeps your mind open to the novelty of unexpected patterns.

So, you see, when you learn, you use the five strategies that build trust. But it also means something more. The new skills or knowledge you have after learning will open new horizons, thus giving hope when it is most needed.

TURMOIL

What happens when you realize what you could have done but didn't? There's a sense of guilt or anger toward others and things, but there's only one person responsible for what you sense. You.

This thought crossed my mind when I saw my student's performance in the last practical class before a test. Some were drifting through the turmoil of formulas, slides, and former exercises instead of thinking about the problem and finding the best way to reach a solution.

Learning an instrument is hard because you have to practice every day. Finishing a puzzle is hard because you have to fit a few pieces every day. Being healthy is hard because you have to exercise and take care of what you eat every day. Learning is no different. Unless you deliberately practice every day, the articulation of knowledge is not a trait achieved by magic. You have to work hard. Every. Single. Day.

You sweat. Get tired. I feel frustrated sometimes and, at other times, exhilarated. It's part of your life and who you are. If you procrastinate and postpone what you have to do to keep developing your learning mind, you postpone the evolutionary opportunity to become more.

Change your mindset and restart.

UNCERTAINTY

The origin of thinking is some perplexity,
confusion, or doubt. (John Dewey)

We already know uncertainty impacts our lives, but what impact does it have on learning?

Learning and thinking are intrinsically connected. The fact thoughts originate a certain state of doubt, hesitation, perplexity - *a state of uncertainty - and induce a self-searching sense to resolve this uncertainty* is what John Dewey defines as *reflective thinking.*

The conflict generated by the state of uncertainty experienced while learning can be disruptive and cognitively demanding, but with the right mindset, it can work as the genesis of knowledge.

The adjustments you make under the disequilibrium experienced in a state of uncertainty are what gives meaning to any learning process. It is what makes it exciting in the first place. Therefore, without elements of uncertainty, learning can be tedious.

The discomfort of uncertainty motivates us to change what we know and believe, bringing our cognitive learning closer to reality and converting it to experiential learning with genuine learning experiences.

Under uncertainty in learning, you're more involved in the process, and this favors a greater awareness of what you learn, making it a rewarding experience.

VALUE

We learn through ideas. Valuing ideas is valuing learning. And valuing the ideas of others means valuing what we learn from them.

The novelty of an idea hides a deeper layer in the puzzle of human knowledge. There's a real insight when we experience the relational side of learning. When we value the ideas of others, we value the inspiration it contains. And often, the best ideas are not ours, or even the others, but the ideas born out of reciprocal valuing of both.

WALKING

A friend told me once - *"We're made for walking."* - and studies show he was right since there is a relationship between moving your legs and a healthy brain.

In May 2018, researchers from the universities of Milan and Pavia showed in the Journal *Frontiers in Neuroscience*[1] an active link between exercise and neurogenesis. When we use our legs, the brain receives vital signals triggering the production of neural cells essential to handle stress and adapt to new challenges in life.

Walking is part of John Medina's first brain rule, which inspired me to change my life, reduce weight, and have a healthier brain. Since I read his book[2] during vacations, I began walking 30 minutes every day. After one year, besides controlling the amount of food on my plate and the amount of sugar, my weight went from 91kg to 75kg without a special diet.

All knowledge workers, such as students, professors, and researchers, are professional thinkers. And we may spend too much time seated in front of a computer without using our legs. Our work depends on thinking, and thinking improves with a healthy brain. Ultimately, taking a walk is *a step forward* in the right direction.

It's time to get up and take a walk.

WELCOMING

We can learn things by ourselves, and we often need to. But when others are involved in our learning process, it's a whole different game.

We could think of others as our learning accountability partners, but the role others may have can be deeper.

We build a life around our relationships with others. Every moment shared with others is an experience teaching us something about ourselves. Sometimes things we need to change, and sometimes things we need to accept as being part of who we are.

Friends, family, colleagues and the next unknown person crossing my path are often the sources of inspiration to learn something new every day. Welcome them warmly.

We may think about renewing learning with pedagogical innovations on how we educate at any age. But, apparently, it doesn't work.

In a recent article, I read a comment about the poor results of an expensive project seeking to evaluate a significant number of pedagogical innovations in schools. The results contained a "dirty little secret."

"That's the dirty secret of all of education research. It is really hard to change student achievement. We have rarely been able to do it. It's harder than anybody thinks." (Barbara Goodson, in *The Hechinger Report*)

Why is it so hard to change how students perform? As a professor, I also wondered about it more than a year ago and formulated a hypothesis. Their achievement depends more on their lives outside school or university than what happens inside a classroom. Then I found confirmation of the reason behind the "dirty little secret,"

> " The problem is that learning is ultimately about changing human behavior, and that is always difficult for adults and children. And so many other things — like nutrition, sleep, safety, and relationships at home — affect learning."

My intuition was in the right direction. Human behavior is behind the success of every human achievement, especially in learning. And any change focused on the results is doomed.

The best way to perform perennial changes in human behavior is through habits. But habits require an identity, a "why." It all starts with finding who we want to be and why. That's the first step. Afterward, we develop the habits related to this "why."

For example, imagine you want to be a writer. If you're focused on publishing a book to be a writer, you may never reach your goal or suffer more than necessary. Instead, when you identify yourself as a writer, you understand that books alone don't make you a writer. Writing does. Thus, it is clear that you need to develop a writing habit because you are a writer, and writers write. Period. Books will come and confirm your identity, not define it.

I think education will change when learning

becomes a habit and a way to live. When you discover why you learn, you will understand why you live—a personal discovery at the core of all learnology.

150

NOTES

ALTRUISTIC

1. Barragan, R. C., & Dweck, C. S. (2014). Rethinking natural altruism: Simple reciprocal interactions trigger children's benevolence. *Proceedings of the National Academy of Sciences, 111*(48), 17071-17074.

CURATION

1. https://9billionschools.org/theblog/2019/1/7/how-to-curate-life long-learning-part-1

DARE

1. Turnwald, B. P., Goyer, J. P., Boles, D. Z., Silder, A., Delp, S. L., & Crum, A. J. (2019). Learning one's genetic risk changes physiology independent of actual genetic risk. *Nature human behaviour, 3*(1), 48-56.

DECLUTTER

1. Ferrari, J. R., & Roster, C. A. (2018). Delaying disposing: examining the relationship between procrastination and clutter across generations. *Current Psychology, 37*(2), 426-431.

FORGETTING

1. https://www.nytimes.com/2019/03/22/health/memory-forget ting-psychology.html
2. Wang, T. H., Placek, K., & Lewis-Peacock, J. A. (2019). More is

less: increased processing of unwanted memories facilitates forgetting. *Journal of Neuroscience*, 2033-18.

MAXIMIZE

1. https://www.dailyinfographic.com/how-to-maximize-way-you-think

MINDSET

1. Crum, A. J., & Langer, E. J. (2007). Mind-set matters: Exercise and the placebo effect. *Psychological Science, 18*(2), 165-171.

MOTIVATION

1. https://hbr.org/2018/12/how-to-motivate-yourself-to-do-things-you-dont-want-to-do

PERENNIAL

1. Candia, C., Jara-Figueroa, C., Rodriguez-Sickert, C., Barabási, A. L., & Hidalgo, C. A. (2019). The universal decay of collective memory and attention. *Nature Human Behaviour, 3*(1), 82.

SLEEPING

1. https://www.wsj.com/articles/can-a-person-learn-while-sleeping-11552744800

SPARK

1. https://www.nytimes.com/2019/03/13/learning/learning-with-when-plasma-becomes-another-fruit-of-the-vine.html

SPIRITUAL

1. Miller, Vachel. "Meaning, purpose, and connection: spirituality in a learning society." *Vimukt Shiksha, Unfolding Learning Societies: Challenges and Opportunities* (2000).

WALKING

1. Adami, R., Pagano, J., Colombo, M., Platonova, N., Recchia, D., Chiaramonte, R., ... & Bottai, D. (2018). Reduction of movement in neurological diseases: effects on neural stem cells characteristics. *Frontiers in neuroscience, 12,* 336.
2. Medina, John. *Brain rules: 12 principles for surviving and thriving at work, home, and school.* ReadHowYouWant. com, 2011.

ACKNOWLEDGMENTS

First and foremost, I would like to thank all readers. You. Only writing makes a writer, but without you, our words do not touch the hearts and minds of those we mean to inspire through words.

Second, I would like to thank all the authors whose words inspire me and keep inspiring.

Finally, I would like to thank my family, whose support and patience enabled me to pursue my dreams of becoming who I think I am.

www.ingramcontent.com/pod-product-compliance
Lightning Source LLC
Chambersburg PA
CBHW051451250726
48655CB00001B/355